W9-DAJ-579

Dennis Smith

FIREHOUSE

Jill Freedman

2

8

Other books by Dennis Smith:
    THE FINAL FIRE
    REPORT FROM ENGINE COMPANY 82

Other books by Jill Freedman:
    CIRCUS DAYS
    OLD NEWS: RESURRECTION CITY.

Photographs by Jill Freedman

Text by Dennis Smith

FIREHOUSE

Doubleday & Company, Inc., Garden City, New York

1977

This book is dedicated to all firefighters
who give so much of themselves in the course of their
calling. Special thanks to all those men who made this
book possible; unfortunately, only some of their images appear
within these pages.

ISBN: 0-385-11585-7
Library of Congress Catalog Card Number 76—23759
* * * * * * * *

Text copyright © 1977 by Dennis Smith
Illustrations copyright © 1977 by Jill Freedman
All Rights Reserved
Printed in the United States of America
First Edition
Designed by Jean-Claude Suarès

I remember sitting, smoke-smudged and beaten, against the grafitti-stained bricks of a South Bronx tenement. Across the street in a burned out, abandoned building the last persistent embers of what had been only minutes before a raging fire were giving up their final wisps in surrender to the firefighters. The job was done, the fire was under control.

A man walked towards me, helmet in one hand, and in the other, hanging as on a hook across his shoulder, was his wet and foul smelling fire coat. He dropped the helmet at my feet and sat beside me, leaning back wearily, throwing the fire coat across his outstretched legs. "God," he said, "I could sleep for a week."

We had been in the fire together sharing the heat and the smoke, and now we were sitting safely together sharing the victory.

I looked at him, at his grime-freckled face. He was smiling. It wasn't an open, felicitous smile, but a small widening of the cheeks and lips in self-satisfaction. He felt good about himself, for he did his job. I felt good about him also, for I could see in him something we see less and less of in America. Here was a working man proud of his work, a civil servant proud of his service, and even a hero proud of his courage, and I silently wished, as I have wished in hundreds of similar circumstances, that I had had a camera.

This firefighter was one of many I have written about over the years, but I knew as I looked at him that I could not adequately describe in writing how he felt about himself, his job, his world. No, this sense of pride, this sense of knowing he has accomplished something worthwhile, this sense of meaningful contribution could have been conveyed much more sensibly, more truthfully, through the camera's lens.

I have since left firefighting in the South Bronx and am now assigned to Ladder Company 61 in the North Bronx, an area where there are fewer false alarms and abandoned buildings. Ladder 61 is relatively quiet when compared to the fire companies of the South Bronx, yet active enough to keep us jumping from one alarm to another. Last year, 1975, Ladder 61 responded to 2,863 alarms, and with each alarm I respond to I still find myself wishing I had a camera, which brings me to the subject of this introduction and the reason for this book—Jill Freedman.

Jill is an award-winning photographer who first came to my attention as she sang, in a clear, lyrical style, an Irish ballad at a small Greenwich Village get-together a few years ago. I remember being im-

pressed then by the range of her voice as I am impressed now with the range of her photographs. She told me that one of her favorite photographs was one she took of a firefighter carrying a kitten from a burning building, and that she had a soft spot in her heart for firefighters because of it. I was of course entertained by this, but because I had been thinking of collecting and publishing a book of photos of firefighters, I was also interested to learn more about Jill Freedman's work.

I made an appointment to see her portfolio of photographs, and after studying it, I realized two things: that I was looking at the work of a unique artist, and if anyone could capture on film the natural pride of that firefighter sitting beside me against a tenement wall, Jill Freedman could.

We then discussed the possibilities of a book of photos of firefighters, but the enthusiasm of the moment soon passed for we were both caught up in other things—Jill putting the finishing touches on her book *Circus Days,* and I on my novel *The Final Fire.*

We next met fortuitously and by chance some time later in Dublin, Ireland where we had both gone on assignment. A friend named Dennis Duggan called my hotel to say that he and Jill had flown over together, and that we should all meet for a drink. We met in the sun-filled drawing room of the Shelbourne Hotel, far from the hazards and brutality of firefighting in the Bronx, and over a genteel Irish tea we discussed what tourists and Irish natives invariably discuss in Ireland—the weather. The conversation though, did progress (there are people who would say regress) to politics and poetry, and finally to writing, photographing, and firefighting. Jill again voiced her enthusiasm for photographing firefighters at work, and we resolved then to do it.

The two of us met in New York a month later with the artist and designer J-C Suarès, whose illustrations on the Op-Ed page of the *New York Times* are known the world over. We agreed that J-C would design the book, I would write the story, and Jill would take the photographs that make this book possible, and meaningful.

I can think of a hundred complimentary adjectives to associate with Jill Freedman's pictures, but words have no real value in relation to photographs. The photographs must stand for themselves, as indeed these photographs do.

Here then, is the story of firefighting as I live it, and the world of firefighting and firefighters as seen by Jill Freedman.

Photography is magic. You catch a moment. You can print it, share it, again and again. Beautiful silver stories. And through it, you can live out your fantasies. Like most kids, I wanted to be a fireman. I guess I forgot about it when I found out I was a girl. I didn't even remember it a few years ago, when I photographed a fireman who saved a cat. But the picture stayed with me, and became one of my favorites. I started noticing firemen a lot more, liking something about them. And gradually I began wanting to photograph them.

I've always admired them. They were for me the antithesis of all the meanness and cruelty you see in the papers and the streets. There was an altruism in the very idea of a fireman that interested me. I wanted to see what they were like. What kind of guy will risk his neck for someone else's? Will run into burning buildings, and feel responsible for every stranger who needs help? You see them sick. Throwing up, passing out, black running out of their noses, even dying. And always coming back for more, welcoming it, playing the fire like a bull. Loving the action. Who are these guys?

They are different than most of us. They are always there when you need them. They care about people all of the time, not just during wars or blackouts or disasters. All of their energy is positive. Their job is to protect people. And so they are always there; they will come when no one else will. People know this, and when there is an emergency they think of firemen. They call them for fights, for accidents, broken pipes, lost kids, no heat, cats up trees, no water, for lonely and sick old people. Frightened people. And they always come. That's their job. No one is afraid of a fireman.

They are like soldiers in that they will die for someone else, or someone else's property. They are not like soldiers in that they will not kill. They are there to help people, not to hurt them. They bring life instead of death. Sometimes they are too late, and they always take it personally. "We lost two," they say. We.

One night we responded to a fire. It was nothing, but there was a lot of smoke and noise. On the way up, a small child with a baby in her arms was standing in her doorway, crying. Her mother was a junkie out hustling. She was alone. And the lieutenant of the truck stopped on his way up the stairs to comfort her. "It's nothin' honey, don't be scared. Go back inside now and lock your door. Everything's all right." A strong man is a gentle man.

They are never sentimental. Drunks are sentimental, and war movies, where people live in the past. A fireman's life is too immediate, too real for sentimentality. They are not modest, but they get a little embarrassed when you say hero. And if you ask one about a rescue he made, he walks away saying he was just doing his job. "That's what I get paid for." And how much do you pay a man's widow when he's bought it?

Because firefighting is the most dangerous job there is. You give it everything, and you take a beating. You have to be fast, and you have to be ready. And you have to know that the other men are, too. And so there's a closeness that grows out of being in combat together. Knowing that your life depends on the man working next to you. Sure that if you're ever in trouble, he's coming for you. Sharing those moments that only someone who has been there can understand.

Like how that black smoke feels in your throat. The panic when your windpipe starts closing. What it's like to be sick from the smells or the pity. The joy of bringing someone back, especially a child. Or failing. The scariness, crawling into blackness, wearing a heavy mask you can't see out of, knowing that when your bell goes off you have to get out. Wondering where out is. The fear. The heat. Burning your ears crawling under beds to rescue dolls. Having it suddenly light up between you and the window. Or on the roof, the stairwell, an incinerator. Can you make it to the ladder, and is it there? The sounds of glass breaking, muffled shouts, somebody's bell ringing somewhere off in the dark. Will you get out in time?

This closeness is especially true of busy companies, which mine were. There's a team spirit you find in a busy company. An excitement. The men look forward to coming into work every day. Sometimes they even come in early. They go nuts during a slow period. Men in busy companies even eat faster, trying to get food down before the next run. If they're having roast beef, cooked nice and pink and juicy, you know for sure they'll have a run. Roast beef is practically a guarantee. Charred and black as their last fire, dry and dull as a false alarm.

They share a firehouse humor, a blunt way of dealing with reality. They love a good laugh, and they need it. And they are sharp. You have to be fast, to be able to take it as well as you give it. They talk straight, and when they're mad they say so, they don't let it build up. There is no time for that. If a man doesn't fit in, he knows it. Each man has a job to do, and he must earn the respect of his group, tough, but fair.

A fireman will tell you he's only doing his job, but it goes much deeper than that. The success of the Emergency Medical Technician Program is a good example. It's voluntary and it takes sixteen weeks, all of it on their own time, not the city's. There is no extra pay or credit, but the men I knew who were in the program jumped at the chance. They went to classes, and they worked in hospital emergency rooms. I saw a fireman I knew from Harlem the other day who was in the program. He told me about two guys from Brooklyn who were studying with him. They responded to a car crash, and when they got there a man was lying on a stretcher with a blanket over his face. The ambulance attendants were standing there smoking cigarettes. "It's all over," they said. One of the firemen found a pulse in the man's neck, worked on him for a long time, and brought him back.

Their interests are as varied as their faces, so are their opinions. Most of them do other things. One night sitting around the kitchen, there was: a guy who breeds orchids; and accountant; an ex-Jesuit; a man going for his law degree, another for his RN; a physics teacher at Stony Brook; a mechanical genius

who could fix anything that used to move.

Some of the times I loved best were sitting around the kitchen after a good job, especially in the middle of the night. The men are tired but exhilarated. It will take a while for them to come down. There is an easy friendship. They joke about little goof-ups and analyze what was good and what could have been better, always thinking, always ready for the next run. Drinking coffee, feeling good about each other, feeling good about themselves. Those were the times I felt closest to them.

So here are firemen as I saw them. New York City firefighters. Not as front page spectaculars, but rather as they are every day, in the firehouse and out on the street. Handsome men, whose boots look good on their legs. Kids trust them. Buffs hound them. Junkyard dogs adopt them. Because they are something special.

Here are real men, and let me tell you, they cry all right. And they joke around, hugging, kissing, and they mean it. They love each other, and boy, is it nice to be around that.

I hope a lot of kids see these pictures. There's no way you can call a fireman a sissy. Let kids see that truly strong men are also soft and gentle; that men can love and respect each other; that being nice instead of nasty makes you feel good. And not a gun

in sight.

Being with firemen re-kindled all kinds of un-realistic dreams. They showed me that not all wars are bad. Wars on rats and roaches aren't bad. Or how about colds? Wars on hunger would be nice, or loneliness; building cities instead of destroying them.

As it is, I saw the only firefights I can respect, fought in the only uniform I like. If men must fight wars, let them fight for life instead of death. Let them fight for their own species, not for other men's ambition or profit. If we must have heroes, then let them be live ones. And if we give out medals, let them be for saving life, not for destroying it.

As one woman in the South Bronx put it, "Thanks, firemen. There's a lot of children live here."

It's a bright, spring morning, and the warm air rushes through the car giving rise to remembrances of springs past. Another winter has gone, and with it the brutal combination of firefighting and cold. In my mind, there is nothing as terrible, for the cold bites into the wet skin as if thousands of metal clamps were attached to the body, and swinging wildly with the wind. Today is a *Puck's Fair* in comparison, and I celebrate it.

Yet, in any weather, firefighting is difficult and dangerous. We are told by those statistic gathering agencies in the nation's capital that firefighting is the most dangerous of all occupations, that more firefighters are killed in the line of duty than miners, police officers, or construction workers, and that the severity rate of our injuries is the highest in the land. We live with these facts by following flag-draped caskets from neighborhood churches, but few firefighters complain about the danger. I remind myself, as the wind splashes refreshingly around me, that ten New York City firefighters have been killed in the past one hundred and twenty days—from burns, from breathing unknown toxic gases, from collapsed floors or caved-in roofs.

I turn off at the Bartow Avenue exit in the Bronx, and I can see the red brick of the firehouse in the

distance. I wonder as I approach if the doors will fly open and I will see the men scurrying around making ready for a response. A fire? A false alarm?

If firefighters do not complain about the dangers inherent in firefighting, they do complain about an ever-increasing workload. The job gets tougher every year.

Most American cities are in financial trouble, and in the haste to trim municipal budgets, fire departments are trimmed arbitrarily, their manpower cut unconscionably, without looking at the realities of firefighting. Mayors demand reductions from all departments, without considering needs or intelligent priorities. And, people suffer from a diminished level of fire protection. If cities are being wrecked, large parts of them are on fire, and it is senseless to reduce the level of fire protection in the middle of the burning.

I pass the doors of the firehouse. Happily they haven't opened—a simple symbol of a safe community, of safe firefighters. The thought occurs, and I laugh at it, that the best fire department is the one that does no firefighting. How much better off a community would be if they paid their firefighter to wait for an alarm without an alarm ever coming. It could be the subject of an Ionesco play.

I park the car in the alleyway next to the firehouse and gather from the back seat my change of clothes, a newspaper, and a container of milk.

The yellow of the stucco walls in the firehouse kitchen looks strangely clean, the grime having been recently removed in preparation for a less significant rite of spring—the department's annual inspection. The men of Ladder Co. 61 and Engine Co. 66 are sitting around two crumb and seed covered oblong tables, breaking open rolls and pallet-knifing butter or jelly across them. One firefighter is talking about the problem of a pay freeze for city employees, and the others are interested.

"I've got six little breadsnatchers at home," he says, "and there's not as much bread as there used to be. And for what? This department expects us to do this kind of work which gets worse and worse every year, and then they want us to take a pay freeze and live on less than what our money could buy two years ago. . . . It's crazy."

The men are more than sympathetic. They are angry. The men of Engine Co. 66 are ragged from work and sleeplessness, having spent the night at a multiple alarm fire.

One of the enginemen places his coffee cup in the sink, and replies, "After I get some sleep I'll tell

you what I think about that, if you've got a few hours to spare. Now, even though it's almost nine o'clock in the morning, I'll say goodnight to you."

"And I'll say good morning to you," I interject.

"Goodnight, good morning. Do any of us know what time of day it is?" That, from a man named Hughie, a rotund, robust man who is on a perpetual diet of starvation and good humor.

Whatever anger the group felt cannot be seen now in their broadly smiling faces.

I put the container of milk in the refrigerator, walk past the rearmount, 100 foot, Seagrave, aerial truck that is Ladder 61, up the stairs, and to my locker. There I change from slacks and sport shirt into the navy blue work uniform of the N.Y.F.D. as the firehouse bells ring out eleven times—the nine o'clock telegraph test signal. There is time before committee work for a cup of tea and a look at the newspaper.

The news is not good. There are rehabilitating drug addicts camped in the City Hall park, detectives are picketing one side of the Mayor's mansion, and a parents group from a local school is picketing the other side. Because of layoffs in the Pest Control office of the Health Department, it is predicted that the city's rat population will double in a year. Prisoners in our newest jail are striking for an increase in food portions. Everyone has a story. Everyone wants a piece of the city.

At nine-thirty, committee work begins in every firehouse in the city, and also in most firehouses throughout the country. It is the ignominious work of building maintenance—washing windows, cleaning toilets and sinks, sweeping and mopping floors, making the beds —which I have always felt should be done by maintenance men. But committee work also means the crucial work of cleaning and maintaining the tools and equipment, making things ready for action, and I've been assigned to check the masks and tools.

There are five of us working in Ladder Co. 61 today, and four in Engine Co. 66. The contracted minimum manning requirements were recently reduced from six men on a ladder company and five men on an engine. Firefighters necessarily suffer in this reduction, but more importantly, the people we serve suffer for they are not getting the level of fire protection they used to get. This is true in most big cities where mayors and city managers are looking to curtail services, just at a time when the country is experiencing an ever-increasing fire problem.

I have spent over a third of my life fighting fires, and a day never passes that I do not feel some frustration over the low regard of fire safety in our country. Do you know that more than 12,000 Americans die each year in fires? That's about 33 lives lost each day. The country's rate of fire per 100,000 population is twice that of Canada, four times that of Great Britain, six times that of Japan. I wonder, really wonder, why the public is not enraged? Perhaps because fire is something we read about in the newspapers, something that happens to "the other guy". Yet, there are more "other guys" in this country than any other.

Just think for a moment of the two hundred thousand Americans that are burned each year, over sixty thousand seriously enough to be hospitalized from two months to two years. Burns are of epidemic proportions, yet are seldom discussed by the news media or government officials. Property damage caused by fire amounts to 3.8 billion dollars each year, and when things like insurance costs and productivity losses are considered, this figure rises to over 12 billion dollars. I can think of these figures every day, for they are part of my life, but how can I calculate the cost of human suffering, the charred loves, the smouldering dreams? I can't.

I take my helmet, coat and boots from the coat rack and place them on the side step of the apparatus, making them ready for an alarm. As I move away, I remember to check that my gloves and flashlight are in the coat pocket. They are.

The masks are kept in a side compartment of the apparatus, and I pull the suitcase-like boxes out and place them on the floor, open them, and begin. Masks are lifesavers, and I check each one thoroughly. The mask weighs about thirty pounds, and I throw each one over my back to check the harness buckles, insure that the rubber face piece fits tightly and double check to see that the air flows through the regulator valve and hose without interruption. I can remember those hundreds of times I could not have gone three or four feet into smoke without this cumbersome piece of equipment on my back. Without it, there would be more parking lots in New York. Next to hose and water, this mask is probably our most crucial piece of equipment, but everything in this business has its hazards, including masks. Because breathing is unrestrained, a firefighter can easily go deeper into heat than might be safe, unknowingly burning his ears and neck.

After checking the air pressure, satisfied that there is at least fifteen minutes of air time in each mask, I close the boxes. As I start to return them to the mask compartment the bells begin to ring. First four bells, then three, another three, then seven. Box 4337, the

intersection of Gun Hill Road and the New England Expressway.

The New York Fire Department, as most fire departments, has an electronic voice alarm system that announces an alarm through a series of loudspeakers in the firehouse. However in the event of a system breakdown the telegraph is the secondary means of communication, and so it is used from 9 a.m. to noon each day to keep the firefighters in touch with the rhythm of the bells.

I step out of my shoes, and into the hip-high rubber boots, folded over below the knee so that they look like the boots the three musketeers wore in pre-revolutionary France. With my leather helmet and rubber turnout coat in hand I step into the riding compartment behind the driver, and behind me steps a man named Brendan. I sit on a small seat placed between the motor housing and a window. On the other side of the motor housing is Hughie, and sitting before him is a man named Jake. Lieutenant Morris sits in the front, next to Billy, the company chauffeur.

The motor roars into my ear, it must be twenty or so decibels over the safe noise level, and, siren blazing, the apparatus moves into the street, trailing behind Engine Co. 66.

Firefighting is separated into two distinct but highly co-ordinated fields of action: engine work and ladder work. The engine firefighters are responsible for dragging hose to the fire and cooling the flames. A fire can exist only if it meets three criteria, commonly called the "fire triangle". These must be fuel, that is, something to burn; heat; and oxygen. To remove one element is to extinguish the fire, and the water from the engineman's hose eliminates the heat by cooling.

The second field of firefighting consists of a team effort to ladder a building, gain entrance to it (called forcible entry, because the building normally must be broken into), search and rescue, ventilate, which is the destructive but necessary act of breaking windows and cutting holes in the roof through which heat and smoke can escape, and overhaul, which is the further destructive, but no less necessary, act of pulling floors up, and ceilings and walls down, to ensure there are no remaining burning embers.

In the fire truck, siren blazing through the hot Bronx streets, I feel confident in being a part of this group of men. With each alarm comes a natural anxiety about the immediate future that is resolved for me simply by looking around at the men I work with.

Firefighters are a close bunch, we keep house to-

gether, eat together, work together, and we are kept close to each other by an interdependency in fires. My life depends on the thinking and action of the guy next to me. I know that, just as he knows his dependency on mine, and we would not be able to operate in the dangerous, dark of heat and smoke unless we understood it.

It is not unusual to see firefighters hugging, kissing, or grab-assing, playful manifestations of love and respect that really say "It's all right, if you need me, I'll be there."

From Gun Hill Road we can see the smoke rising from the New England Expressway underpass. Traffic on the expressway is already backed up for as far as we can see in either direction. We will have to go up along the service road and drop a ladder down the thirty or so feet to the expressway.

The contents of a large transport truck are burning, and as we lower the aluminum extension ladder, I can see the truck driver working desperately to save some of the cargo. But time is against him, the fire has grown so intense that he must move away. Strewn on the roadway are large fans, the body of a dragon, kettle drums, beautifully inscribed silk kimonas, and other property of the Japan Folkloric Dance Company. The driver saved a little, but most of it is lost to the flames, for the truck is now a fireball.

Jake and I climb to the roadway, and buttress the ladder for the engineman and the hose. Jake is carrying a six foot hook and a $2\frac{1}{2}$ gallon, pressurized water extinguisher. The water can will not be used for the fire is too great. It would be like spraying a garden hose into a cyclone. I am carrying a four pound axe, and another six foot hook.

The enginemen advance the hose line, extinguishing the fire, as Jake and I pull the wooden crates from the truck bed. We do what we can until the fire is safely diminished, and then we climb into the still smoking truck, and between coughs, push the charred and falling-apart crates to the roadway.

The driver meanwhile has sat on the edge of one of the saved crates, his hands and nose blistered with burns, and begins to sob uncontrollably. Hughie consoles him, and treats his wounds.

There are consequences to a fire that firefighters seldom see, when those who are victimized begin to put the pieces back together again.

The driver mumbles that he has driven the property of the dance company thousands of miles, from city to city on their American tour, and he asks why this had to happen to him. The dance company was to perform next in New Haven, but how will they do the

Dance of the Great Snake of Yamata without the dragon's body, how will they do the Dance of the Temple Maiden without their fans and geisha costumes, and how will they do the Dance of the Rice Planting without their drums?

An ambulance comes for the driver, and after pulling the planking from the interior truck sides to make sure there are no residual embers, we take a last look at the pile of debris that was once the pride of Japan's Folkloric Dance Company. I wonder if the show will go on? Will I ever know?

Again in the firehouse, I wash the soot from my face and go to my next duty. The tools.

There are four tools that are as fundamental to a ladder company's work as a ruler is to a draftsman: the four-pound axe, the six-foot hook, the circular power saw, and the thirty-inch long halligan tool, a steel prying tool named after its inventor that has a three-inch spike and a perpendicular adze at one end, and a prying fork that looks much like a straightened nail remover at the other. These are the tools of forcible entry, ventilation and overhauling work, and are also used to chop down doors or break through walls to effect rescue.

We carry four six-foot hooks, two ten-foot hooks, and one that is twenty-feet long, used exclusively for high ceilings. The handles are wooden, and the steel ends which are pointed and hooked, looking somewhat like a fleur-de-lys, halved up the middle, are used to pull ceilings and walls down. The six-foot hooks were used at a fire last night, and I'll have to clean them. After laying them on the floor next to a small hose, I go to the kitchen for soap and steel wool.

The men of Engine 66 are sitting around, having a last cup of coffee before beginning their assigned housecleaning. A man is shoveling butter onto a roll, and another named Frankie says, "C'mon, will you, save me some butter."

Another man says, "I didn't think Puerto Ricans used butter."

Still another says, "No, lard. If we only had some lard."

Frankie responds, "It's all right, fellas, use all the butter you want, 'cause I just lost my appetite. But I'll get even."

Banter is endless in the firehouse, a manifestation of the closeness in firefighting. If a man is excluded from the joking, it is because he, in some way, has excluded himself and the teamwork of the fire company will probably suffer. Fortunately, everyone in this firehouse at one time or another becomes a target.

I begin to tiptoe out of the kitchen, but a voice stops

me. "Oh oh, Dennis is stealing Brillo pads again."

"No," I say, "the tools gotta be cleaned, and anyway a little *hard work* will never hurt you. It keeps you in shape."

"Keeps you in shape, huh," a man says, the same who was shoveling the butter, "did you ever take a look at the great philosophers? They were all fat and ugly, and lived 'til ninety. You work hard and keep in shape. Me, I'm looking forward to the geriatric ward, hands shaking, tapioca pudding dripping from my chin, tapping rendezvous signals on the wall with my cane to the perky grandmother in the next room."

I have often been asked if my relationships with the men I work with have changed since I became a writer of books. They haven't really. There are no special privileges or considerations in the firehouse to keep me apart from them. The firehouse is not a democracy of the elite, but a social situation where one is accepted and respected for his contributions to the job. I once worked with a man who was an avowed Marxist, a philosophic anathema to most firefighters, but this man was fearless at fires and a willing worker in the firehouse, and so was admired by the men he worked with. Yet, he never wavered in his belief that capitalism is the root cause for the poverty and deprivation of places like the South Bronx, and the rest of the men remained intransigent in their opposition.

The firehouse can be like that, a center where divergent views and personalities come together around the job, where men, no matter who they are or what they think, can love each other for what they do.

Still smiling, I scrub the tools with the Brillo and wash them down. A man walks by carrying a shopping bag.

"What's our pleasure today, Frankie," I call out.

"Flank steak à la rouge," he answers.

"A la rouge?"

"Would you expect à la blue or à la green in a firehouse?"

"No," I say, "I guess not."

It will be another hour until lunch, and the beds have to be made, the bathrooms cleaned, and the floors mopped. As I begin to climb the stairs, the voice alarm blasts, and I run to the apparatus. The fire engines scream, and we are off.

All is still at the corner of Burke Avenue and 233rd Street. A false alarm, one of over two hundred and twenty thousand that New York firefighters will respond to this year. It's crazy. Inexplicable. The men sigh in frustration, but say nothing. We have become conditioned to false alarms.

When I was a kid, even the toughest misanthropes of my neighborhood would not consider sending a false alarm. It was dishonorable then, in a curious sort of way, an action that was simply unacceptable to us all. But false alarms have become a way of life to today's underprivileged youth. The neighborhood of my youth was underprivileged enough, and I resent like hell the change in attitude toward false alarms, the law, and authority, by kids who have come to think they deserve more from life, from you and me, simply because they exist. False alarms, born not simply of poverty and deprivation, but of a court system that coddles criminals, politicians who float with Dante's trimmers, indifferent and ignorant parents, and a pervasive psychology that says cities have become indecent—places to abuse and destroy like old toys.

Back at the firehouse, the committee work continues. Some of the beds are remade, the others have not been slept in and are left as they are for tonight's crew.

The sound of the bells blankets the firehouse again, and we are off. This time there is a fire in the incinerator shaft of one of the twenty-five high-rise buildings in the Co-op City complex. While the shaft size meets the building code standard, it is too small to be practical, and boxes or large bags of garbage can become lodged between the shaft walls. Something has become lodged there, between the sixteenth and seventeenth

RIP
L-31

FIRST IN OUR HEARTS
SECOND IN THE BRONX
TENTH
L-38

floors, and garbage has accumulated to the rim of the incinerator door on the seventeenth floor. The incinerator furnace in the basement had been lighted, and the heat rose up to the accumulated garbage, igniting it. It is another rubbish fire, and like false alarms, a needless waste of our time. If the builders had spent another few dollars on bricks and made the shaft wider, we would not be here ten or twelve times a week for similar fires.

But the smoke is thick on the sixteenth floor, for it has banked down from the garbage above, and something must be done. The angle of the incinerator door is much like the door of a postal box, cut at a 45° angle, and we cannot get our tools into the shaft to pull the garbage or to push it down. The Lieutenant tells me to get a brick and drop it down the shaft from the roof, thirteen floors above.

Unfortunately, we are not issued bricks, we do not store bricks on the apparatus, and so I will have to conjure one up. I've done it before, and it quite frankly makes me feel a little guilty. The only bricks in the neighborhood that are not mortared down and shaped into buildings are those that rim the planting square for the trees that line the Co-op City streets. They are handsome, granite stones shaped like cobblestones and weighing about thirty pounds each. They are geometrically arranged in the dirt surround-

ing the trees, and almost every square patch has a gaping hole where a firefighter has stolen a brick to drop down the incinerator, to free burning garbage that became lodged in a shaft that was impractically built. It is another small illustration for me of a world that is not going quite right.

I take the elevator to the street, and with a six-foot hook dislodge a stone from the dirt. I carry it to the roof, climb a short iron ladder, and dump it down the chimney-top of the shaft. The thirty pounds of dead weight impacts upon the garbage, frees it, and the job is done. Twenty minutes have passed since we received the alarm, and it is fortunate that another more consequential alarm wasn't sounded during that time. False alarms and nuisance fires rob the public of our fundamental value—that of being on call, being ready, when a life is endangered.

The committee work is being completed in the firehouse. The bathroom sinks and commodes have been brushed clean, and I take a mop to the floor. The incongruity does not escape me. I do resent this a little, City managers presume it is natural for a firefighter to mop his floors, while they don't presume it natural for, say, a school teacher. The fire fighter, in my mind, is ill-thought of in this regard.

The alarm bell rings twice, the time signal telling us it is noon. Soon thereafter the shout of "chow down" is heard, and we all head toward the kitchen and the "steak à la rouge." It looks less pretentious than its title, flank steak on Italian bread, topped with onions, boiled in a mixture of catsup and water, but it's tasty and we all eat rapidly, hoping to beat out the next alarm.

Jack, who had volunteered to cook the meal, was complimented, and Frankie, who had gone to the store to buy it, was duly paid: $1.50 from each man. Ten men ate a meal that cost $14.00, and the extra dollar was put into a collection can for the Firefighters Burn Center, which is a group of firefighters working to create a major burn center in New York City. Our firehouse must donate about $50 a month.

I go into the television room which had been an equipment room and done over, to watch the tail end of the noon news. A mosaic on one wall has been made with multi-colored carpet samples. It is a comfortable room, built and paid for by the firefighters, for the city of New York cares not at all about the amenities of fire houses. Firehouses are classic illustrations of the old maxim: God helps those who help themselves.

Billy, the chauffeur, is sitting in a corner reading a paperback novel, and I sit on a couch, watching the television as I thoughtlessly flip through a magazine.

The time is my own until our drill period at two o'clock, or, of course, until an alarm comes in. And, of course, an alarm does come in, just as I see a story in the magazine that interests me. Billy, the chauffeur, throws the novel down, saying, "God, or someone, doesn't want me to ever finish this book." Well, I say to myself while running to the apparatus, we did get through the meal without an alarm.

The alarm is serious this time. It is at the north end of our district, again by the New England Thruway. The traffic is again backed up for miles, and as we enter the Thruway, the truck jumps the curb and rides the grass to the scene of the accident.

It looks as though a car hit the side railing on one side of the highway and caromed to the other side, hitting a light post head-on. A young boy, about seven, was evidently thrown from the car, and run over by a passing car or truck. He is dead, and his body is not in one piece. It is a sad, gruesome job, but it has to be done, and the men begin to put the pieces of this small human being in one place, while I and others run to the car to check the driver. It is a woman, his mother I guess, semi-conscious and delirious. There are four or five empty beer bottles on the back flooring, and I wonder if the woman had just drunk them? I wonder if she had been driving while drunk, and caused the death of this little boy? The boy, I observe, is not much smaller than my own sons, but I don't know what to make of that fact.

This can be a soul-searching job, filled with what-if's, and while I realize that open beer bottles in a car mean nothing in themselves, I can't help thinking that this waste of life is someone's fault. Whose, I don't know. The mother's, the beer company's, the bottler's, the car company's, the highway construction company's? We never learn the answers on the rescue side of tragedy.

The ambulance comes, and the boy is wrapped in a canvas bag. The mother is tied onto a stretcher and lies unknowingly next to her son as the ambulance sirens away. The glass and blood on the highway are hosed away, and the traffic begins to move again.

It is time for drill in the firehouse. Each day at 2:00 in every city firehouse, a one-hour period is spent discussing and practicing the way we do things, everything from handling an axe, to first-aid, to ladder placement, to ventilating a fire. Today, we will practice the rescue knot, used to carry a firefighter down the side of a building to a windowsill rescue. Lt. Morris first talks about the rope: it is made of fiber into yarn, into strand, into rope, weighs 35 pounds, and is 150 feet long. We use it to effect res-

cue, to transport tools and equipment to building roofs, to support suction hoses, and to tie anything to anything. "Okay," Lt. Morris says, "I need a volunteer to tie the rescue knot. Dennis, you'll do fine."

"Man," I reply, "you don't even give everyone else a chance to step backwards."

"All right," Lt. Morris laughs, "everyone else take one step backwards and give Dennis a chance to volunteer."

More small banter. It makes the time pass more interestingly, it gets the job done.

I take the end of the rope and measure one and a half arm's length, fold the rope, make a bowline on a bight knot, spread the two circles of rope and step into them. Lt. Morris makes a half hitch and places the extension of the rope under my arms and around my chest and ties the end. I am now fully supported within the rope, and ready to be lowered from a roof top to a victim waiting at a window below.

I've seen this knot and this procedure used at fires several times, and it is important, it does save lives. Each of the men goes through the procedure, step by step. We have all done it, perhaps hundreds of times, yet we understand that in a life-saving business like ours, there is no such thing as too much practice.

With the drill over, I go to the kitchen to boil water for tea, and search for a piece of bread leftover from lunch. I stop there to have a searching look at the bulletin board. As in the military, firefighters are accustomed to look over the bulletin board once a day. There are multitudinous union notices pinned up, notifications of company dinners and picnics, newspaper clippings of recent fires, a small card advertising four snow tires for sale, and a *New Yorker* cartoon. The cartoon pictures two men walking through a forest, one saying to the other, "Look at it this way Leroy. If your book was a best seller, they would have to chop all this down." One of the firefighters had crossed out Leroy, and penned in Dennis. I laughed.

The kettle whistles and I make the tea, and sit in front of a lone piece of bread. A few of the men have also poured tea or coffee and sit beside me. The talk is not much different from that of men grouped together at a neighborhood bar: sports, kids, a good-looking woman, cars, the weather, other places one might like to be. The small difference is that words like FIREMAN and CHIEF and FIREHOUSE pop in every few sentences.

After spreading jelly on the bread, I take one bite, and the voice alarm bellows through the room. We move out quickly and in less than three minutes we are at the south end of Co-op City, where the building complex stops and the railroad tracks begin. A young boy is lying by the fire alarm box, having been dragged there by friends. He had climbed the six-foot fence and then climbed on top of a railroad power shack. A small boy, black, and about nine years old, he had touched the wrong wire and was severely shocked and burned. So much electricity ran through his body that there are quarter-sized holes that had burned through the bottom of his sneakers, and the top layer of black skin had been burned back on one arm to his shoulder, exposing the off-white second layer of skin. His legs and shoulders are severely burned, but the boy does not cry, or even whimper. He looks around, in shock, without really recognizing any of us.

The men of Engine 66 administer to him, as their Lieutenant calls for an ambulance. There is not much we can do, for we don't have proper medical supplies. All of us feel the futility of knowing what to do but not having the wet gauze to cover his wounds. There is a new, life-saving burn covering, recently invented, that not only keeps bacteria from entering the wound, but kills the existing bacteria there. We had been talking in the firehouse about it just recently, but the words and the knowledge have no value here, no meaning. The stuff is what we need, the stuff to save a life. But it won't come, and even though there are trained and registered nurses and emergency medical technicians among us, we are not equipped for emergencies that require medical treatment. It is ironic, for we do carry stretchers. We can carry away victims, but we can't help them.

The men of Engine 66 put a folded blanket under his head, and keep the swelling crowd back as we are called on the radio for another alarm. As we pull away, I ask Jake, who is sitting across from me, "Do you think he'll make it?"

Jake shakes his head, saying, "If he knows how to fight hard."

The alarm is false, and we return to the firehouse. But the truck does not back all the way in before we are called again to an alarm. It is on 233rd Street, and since we are not assigned on the first alarm, we have been special called. The assigned truck must be at another box. Perhaps a false alarm?

We can see and smell the smoke blocks away. A group of "taxpayers" (the name we've given one-story light commercial buildings) is on fire. There are three stores: a bar, a dry cleaners, and the last is vacant. The fire has extended fully through the bar, and through the cockloft (the common space between

the ceiling and the roof) to the dry cleaners.

The men of Engine Company 72 already have water on the fire as we pull up. We put masks on, for we know that we will have to go inside as soon as we're able to pull the ceilings down, and looking a little like amphibians, we go from store to store, breaking the windows, creating ventilation for the heat and smoke.

The powerful water streams quickly extinguish the visible flames, and as we are about to enter the smoke-filled bar, the Battalion Chief orders us to back away. There is a three-ton air conditioning unit on the roof, and fire has so weakened the structure that the collapse of the roof is probable, if not inevitable.

We are not anxious to go in anyway, for there is no obvious life hazard, except perhaps our own. We lost a firefighter in the borough of Queens just weeks ago in a similar fire. The roof and the air conditioning unit crushed him.

Ladder 51 has put their tower ladder (a large tele-scoping platform) to work, and the water pours from their pretzel-shaped, stang nozzle as if from a water cannon. They manipulate the tower ladder above the building, and shoot the water down on the fire that has now burned through the roof. Soon a smoke cloud rises up and they are lost in it, taken from our view. The wind pushes, and the smoke clears a little, but as quickly, the men are engulfed again by the smoke. Why would anyone want to do that for a living, I ask myself. And not a terrific living, at that.

Finally the roof caves in, but only partially. One side of it remains horizontal. Still, the ceilings must be pulled down, and the fire extinguished in the cock-loft. If not, it could burn for hours.

The Chief orders us into the bar, and I curse silently as I look up at the ceiling. It is made of impressed tin, and the most difficult of all ceilings to pull down.

"Just our luck," Hughie says.

There is no point in replying, for the job has to be done. Hughie has brought a ten-foot hook, and we throw it into the ceiling, and pull together. Hughie is a big man, and our combined strength makes just a little rip in the tin. It's like tearing a one-inch strip of paper from a billboard. But we continue, little by little, inch by inch, until a hole is big enough to shoot water through. All the while, lead drippings are falling from the tin seams, and molten tar comes from the roof as if from a spigot. The firefighters move in with the hose, and shoot the water through our well-earned hole in the ceiling. They then back out, and we continue to pull on the hook.

Hughie's mask begins to ring, signalling that he has only three minutes of air left in his tank. The smoke has lifted a little, though, and Hughie and I back out to remove the masks. On the street, I can see three firefighters carrying out another firefighter from the dry cleaning store.

"The ceiling came down on a couple of them," a passing man says to Hughie.

I silently ask myself again, as Hughie and I re-enter the store, why would anyone want to do this job for a living, or why would men want to volunteer to do this in smaller towns?

We begin to pull again on the hook, smoke and ashes rapidly covering our faces so that you could almost write on them, as on a dirty window. The job has to be done and we pull and pull and pull until it seems my arms are no longer attached to my shoulders. Every now and then the enginemen move up with the hose and give our ever-widening hole a splash, and we continue unil almost half the ceiling is down. Our officer speaks to the Chief, and the Chief agrees to give us a few minute's rest. Going out to the street is a little like getting off an airplane in Miami.

Hughie, Jake, Brendan and I sit on a curb across the street from the fire. We are soiled men. Dirty, tired, and not willing to speak much, we look at the fire, and at the working firefighters. It is at times like

these that I know the answer to why men choose to do this for a living. It is simple, perhaps too simple to say, that we like ourselves and we like each other for what we-do. But simple or not, that is the answer.

Three men have been taken to the hospital from this fire, but the fire is still being fought.

It is always at the risk of self-aggrandizement that I write about firefighters, but I try to think of myself as a recorder of action, of the firefighter's work, and I cannot think of firefighters in action without realizing that they are truly unique human beings, being able to persevere through the greatest hardships of heat and smoke, and get the job done. They are courageous without thinking about courage, and humble to a man, about what they do. Perhaps it is this humility that I see in the men around me that makes me apprehensive to shout their merits. I should learn by their example.

Yet, as I sit on a city curb, stinking with the smell of smoke, there is an easy swelling within me, knowing that I am a part of all I see. These men are the last American pioneers, for they face, with each day, with each fire, an uncertain future. There is no certain predictability about our fires, except that they will burn until the firefighters extinguish them.

We've been sitting perhaps a little too long, and Brendan suggests we go back into the smoke and give some others a break.

It is still smoky and hot, but our hooks go to the ceiling in studied regularity. Up, push, pull, pull. It goes like that until my arms stop feeling altogether. Most of the ceiling is down, and most of the fire extinguished, but there are still patches of flame in the corners of the collapsed part of the roof.

It is nearing six o'clock now, and the Chief orders us to "take up", to leave the fire and return to the firehouse. The fire, although still burning, is under control. The night crew will return to do the overhauling work.

In the firehouse shower, I soap my hands well, and then shove my soapy fingers into my nostrils. The fingers come out black, and I resoap them and repeat the action until the nostril walls are clean. The corners of my eyes, and my nails will be cleaned when I return home. Washing after a day at the firehouse is ritualized for me, for it is the symbol of hard work and the satisfaction that comes with it. Accomplishment comes with getting grime-covered in a fire.

While dressing, I can see Billy, the chauffeur, leaning back on a chair against his locker, reading his book. Perhaps he will finish it tonight.

Brendan enters the locker room, and begins to

dress. I'm just packing my wet clothes into my shoulder bag as he says, "What do you think about that kid?"

"Which kid?" I ask.

"The kid that got burned there."

"That kid. He was pretty bad. I don't know."

"Yeah," Brendan says, "I don't know either. Jees, I hope he makes it."

I am driving home through a clear evening light, thinking of the day. The thought comes, that the point about firefighting is that we don't have to know the answers. It is enough to do your best.

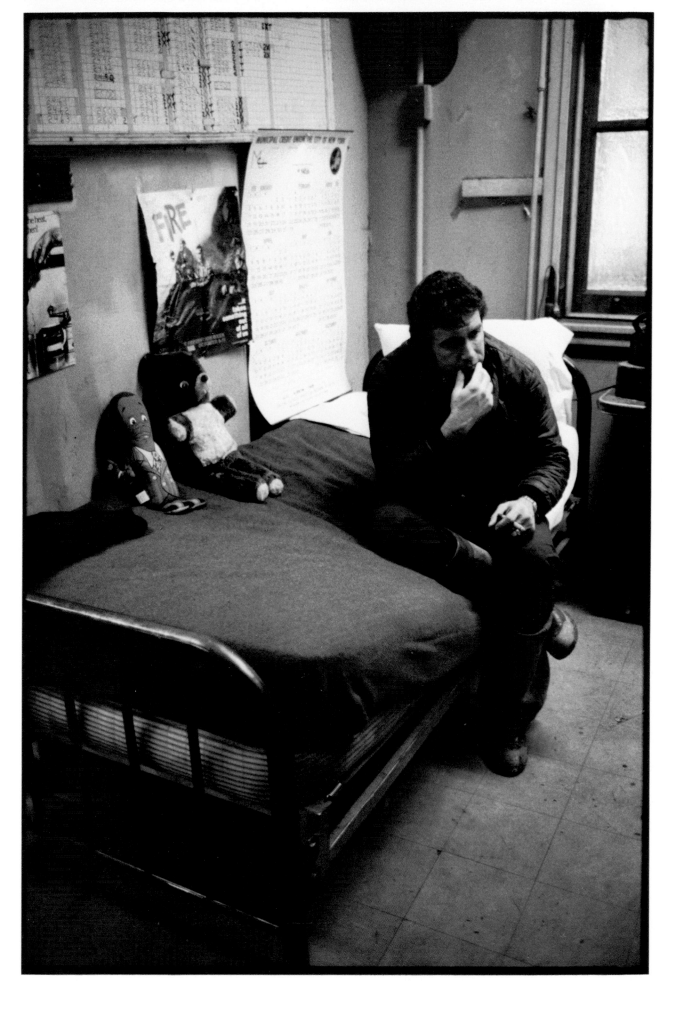

48 **"There is an innocence about firefighting, as there is about mountainclimbing, or growing up."**

54   **"The destruction is often an insult to someone's labor."**

64

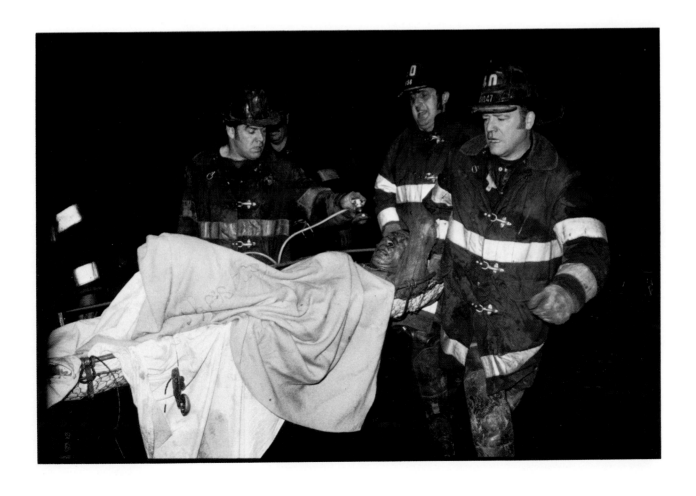

"There are firefighters who have become so conditioned to fires that they wouldn't walk an extra block to see one."

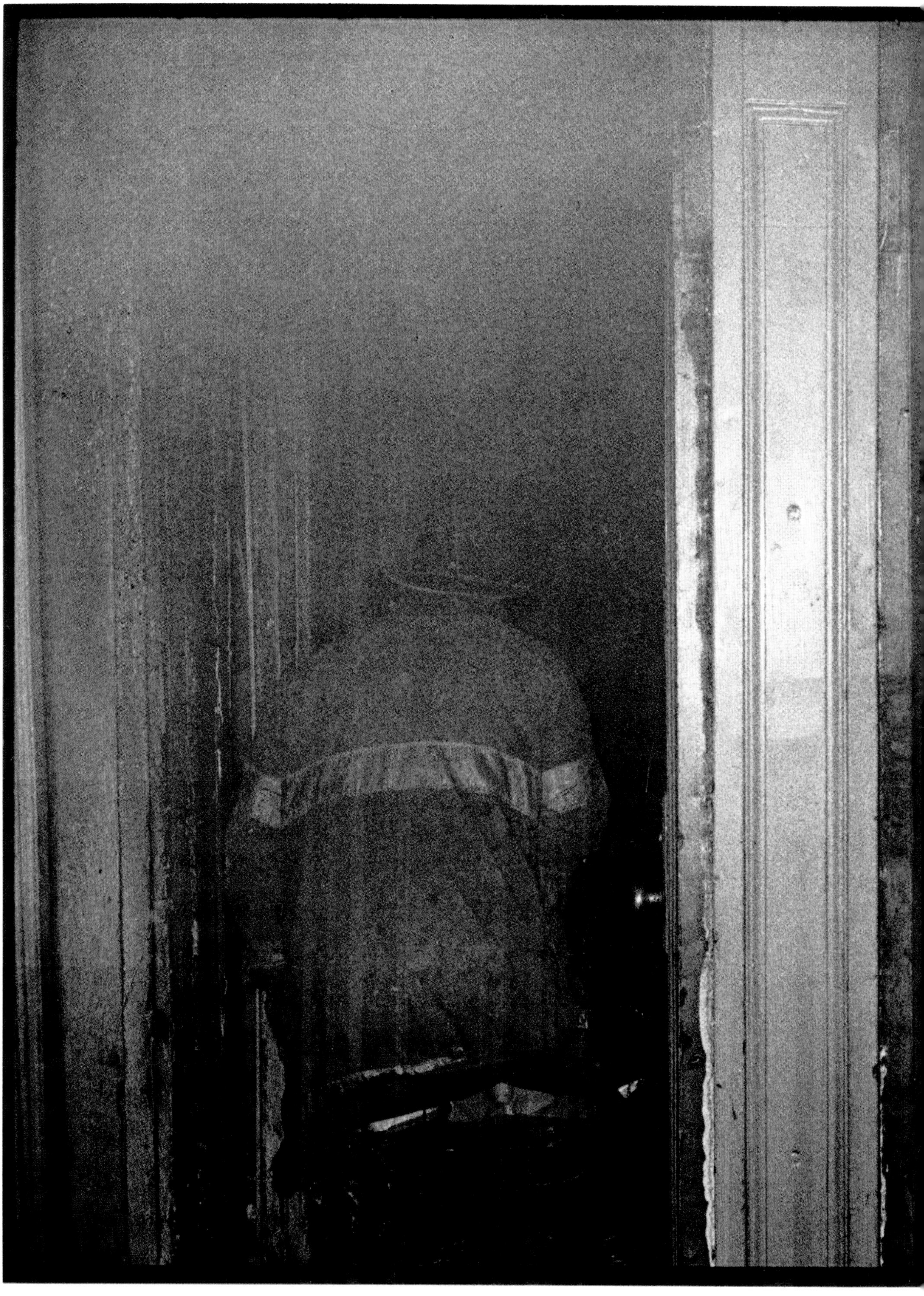

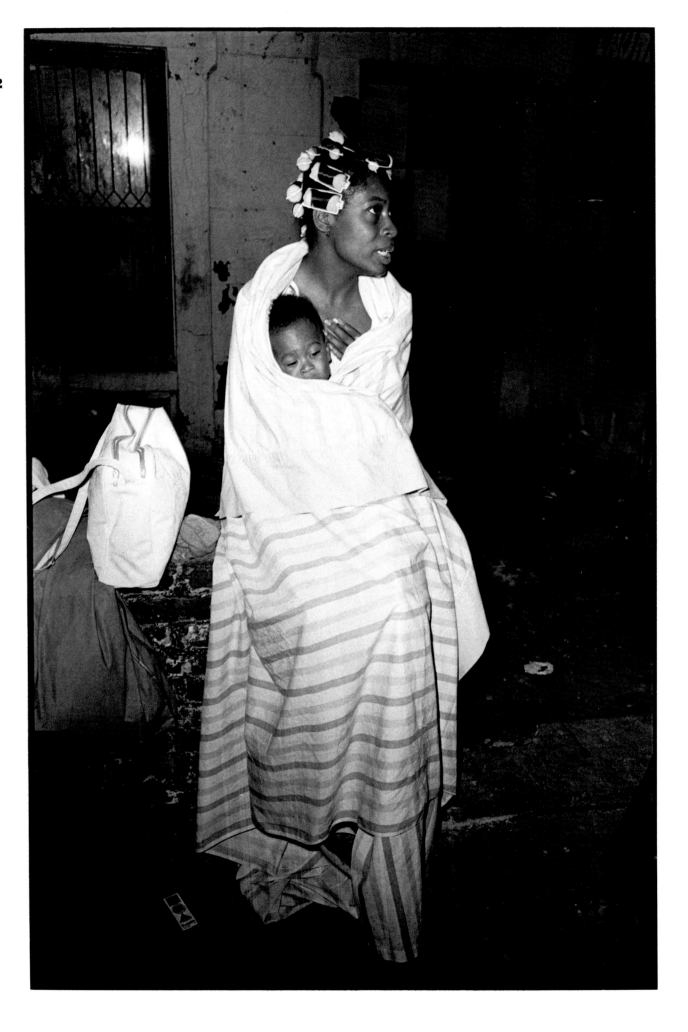

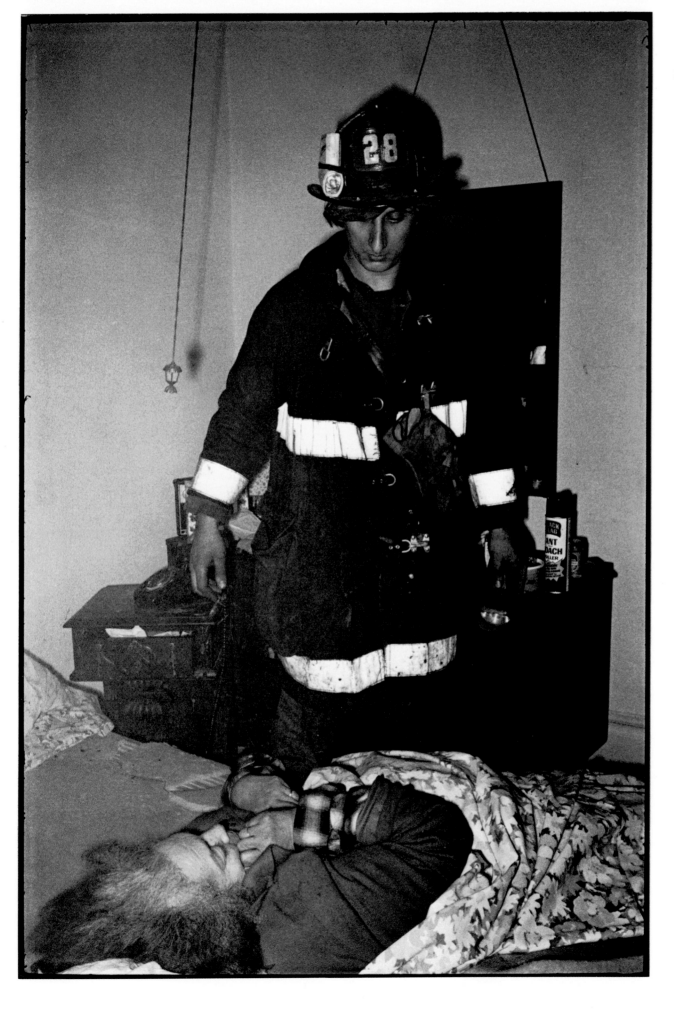

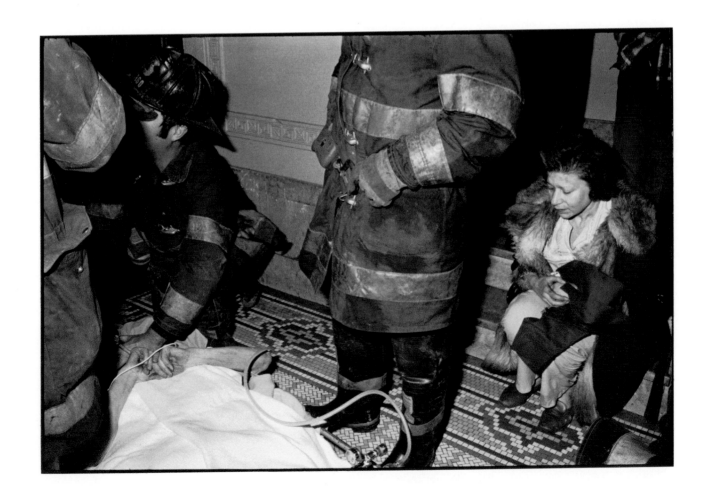

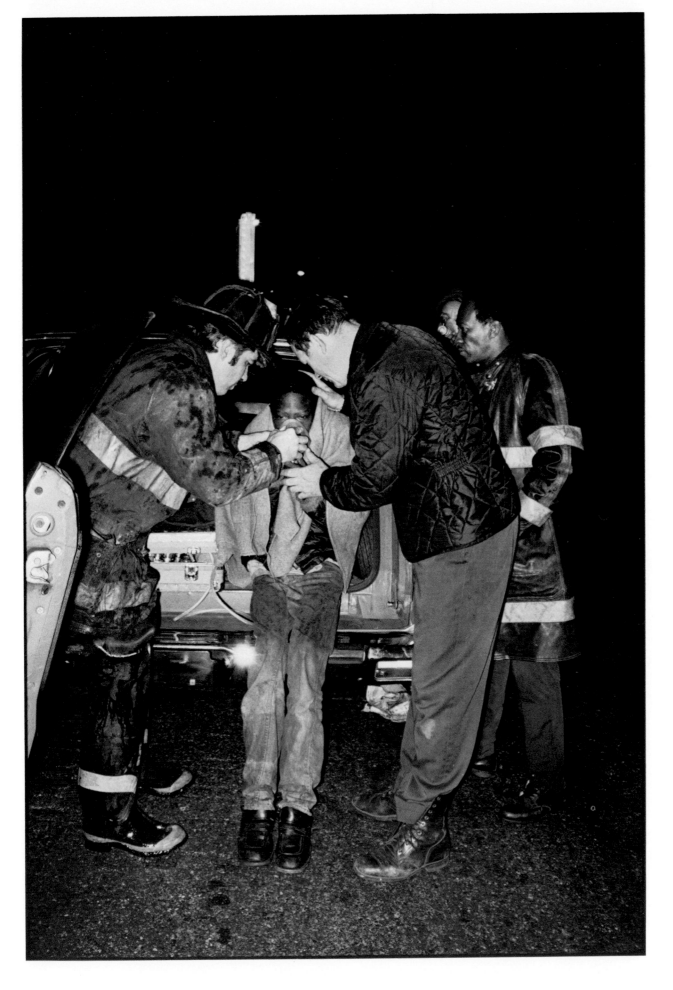

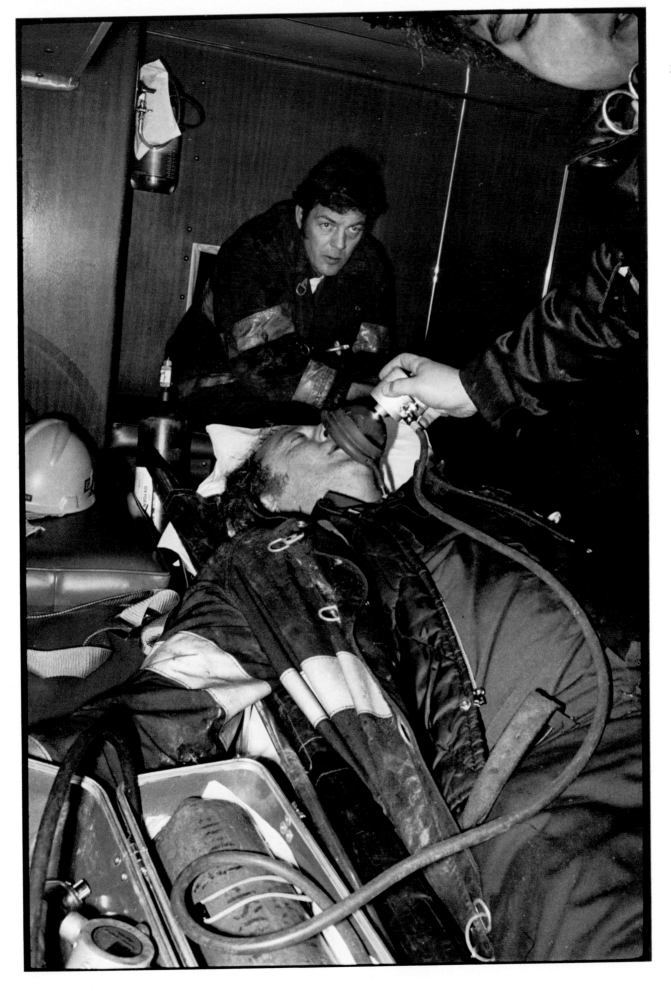

130 "More firefighters are killed while in the performance of their work than miners, construction workers, or police officers, and the severity rate of our injuries is the highest of all occupations."

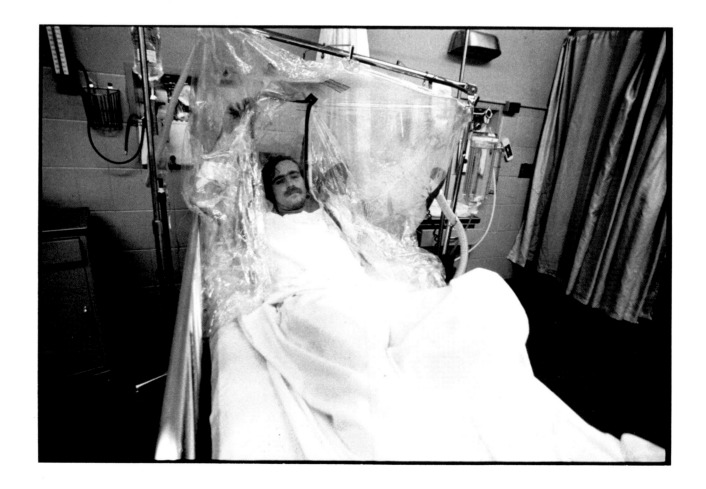

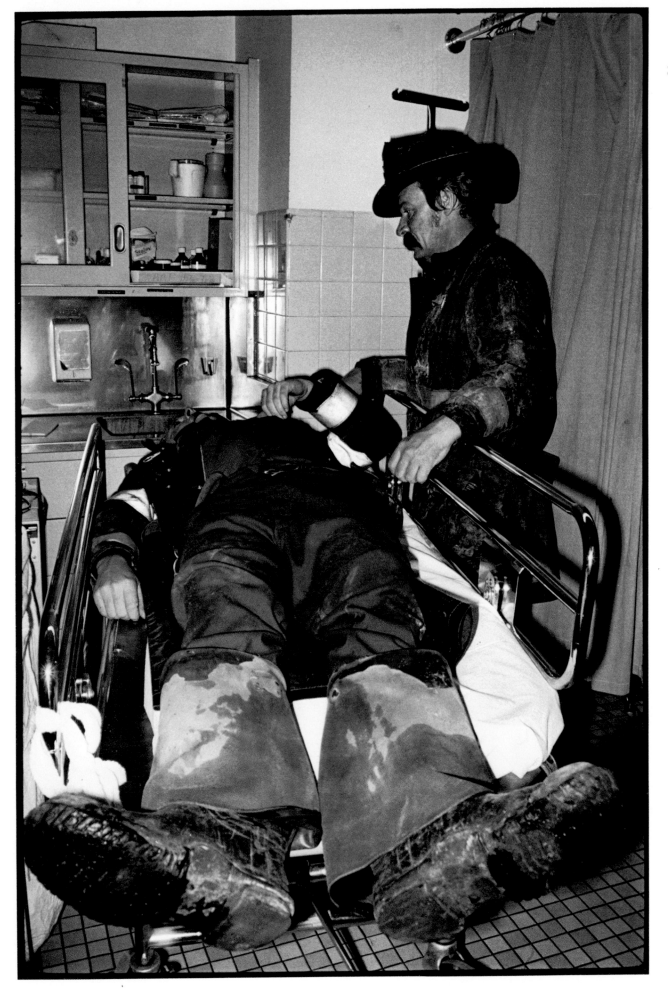

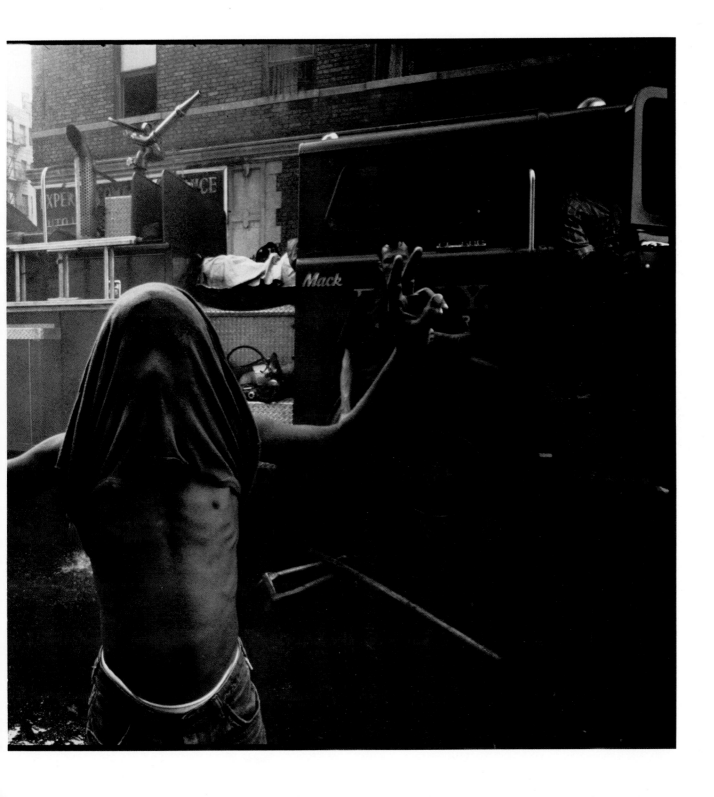

144 "You do the best you can. You put the fire out, and wait for another one. The night is always young in firefighting."